Sourcing Smarts

Keeping it Simple with China Sourcing and Manufacturing

Edith G. Tolchin
with Don Debelak
and Eric Debelak

Sourcing Smarts: *Keeping it Simple with China Sourcing and Manufacturing.*

Printed in the United States of America.

www.sourcingsmarts.com
www.sourcingsmartsinchina.com

ISBN 978-0-615-20411-6

Cover Design by Josh Wallace,
www.joshwallace.com

Table of Contents

Preface

This book is dedicated to all the innovators who have tirelessly persevered through endless rejection, to reach their goals of sharing their marvels with the world. There are so many great ideas out there and so many people who can't figure out what to do with them. Hopefully reading this book will help make it a little easier for the next generation of Einsteins, Salks and Franklins to bring their inventions to market. Perhaps "Sourcing Smarts" can help locate the yet-untapped talents of future generations.

This book is also dedicated to the memory of my late husband and guardian angel,

Donald Tolchin, who always supported and believed in me, from the early days of EGT Global Trading. I will be eternally grateful because not everyone gets to experience the love of a lifetime. He was truly my knight in shining armor.

Last, I thank my children, Dori and Max Freeman, each for being beautiful souls, and for teaching me patience and tolerance. Their wisdom has made me realize how much a mother can learn from her babies!

Edie Tolchin - 2008

Chapter 1

To Source or Not to Source

You have a great invention. You've done lots of research, have a patent or patent-pending status and a working prototype. You have made several unsuccessful attempts at licensing, and have decided you might like to consider manufacturing on your own so you can have better control of sales and marketing.

Now, the big question .....

Should you source your product in China?

Many factors should be considered before sourcing in China. I will list the cons first, and then the pros.

<u>Cons</u>:

1) Difficult Communication

2) Quality and Accessibility

3) Delivery Delays

4) Minimum Order Quantities

<u>Pros</u>:

1) Improved Workmanship

2) Attitude - business relationship

3) New Jobs in USA

4) PRICING!

<u>Cons</u>:

1) <u>Difficult Communication</u>: If you are not experienced in corresponding with China or Taiwan, your first

attempt – typically by e-mail nowadays – may be very trying. Although the office personnel at most Asian factories do speak English, it is not the same "English" that we speak here in the USA. Many do not understand our local idioms or jargon, so remember to keep it simple and do not commit to anything you do not understand. Best-case scenario: Pay a little more and hire a translator, or use an international trade consultant who specializes in working with Asian factories.

2) <u>Quality and Accessibility Often Depend on the Type of Product</u>:

Many Asian factories produce excellent quality sewn and textile items. Their workers can be very talented and creative. However, forget about specialty fabrics or matching prints that you found in the USA. It can be done, but your costs will escalate if you have custom-made fabric prints produced in China. You should also be aware that typically, the best grades of cotton are not found in China or Taiwan. But what about electronic inventions? Very high quality. Printing for packaging is not great, but has been improving over the years. The bottom line is – you really need to see counter-samples before committing to a purchase order. If your product must be specially made with a mold or tooling, first ask to see samples of similar stock items the factory has produced so you can be sure they can achieve the quality and workmanship you are looking for. Always arrange for production testing with an independent safety/testing lab (more info on this to follow in Chapter 2). Always ask for references … and *always* check them!

3) Delivery delays: There will be many delays – especially for first orders – from the time you submit your

prototype and the factory sends you back a counter-sample. Be prepared to go "back and forth" by e-mail numerous times before quality control issues are ironed out. You might find, for example, that a button is on the wrong side, a light bulb must be larger, printing needs to be darker, or the outer box has to be thicker. It's also important to know that during their holidays many Asian factories may close for two weeks or more (as with the Chinese New Year festival), which could delay your shipment. Ask if they can provide you with their holiday schedule so you are aware well in advance of their down times. Also, during typhoon/monsoon seasons everyone is on watch for delays. If you are told that your delivery will be 30-45 days, figure more like 60-75 days, allowing for holidays, coordinating pre-production and mass-production samples, independent testing, etc.

4) MOQs (Minimum Order Quantities): You might have heard that sourcing in Asia requires you to purchase huge quantities, and this can be difficult if you are just starting out and merely want to "test the waters" with your product. For many industries the quantity rule holds

true. For most new products, the factory itself must source the components for your new invention from several different factories that in turn issue an MOQ to your factory for their products. So, that is why sometimes you must purchase large quantities (50,000 vs. 5,000 pieces). In the textiles industry this can frequently happen. With each new invention that is sourced, in order to make a counter-sample and provide you with a price quote, the factory must get quotes on components such as zippers, buttons, ribbons, thread, fabric, packaging, and labels. Each of your factory's suppliers has an already-established MOQ. So, as you can see, it is not easy for the factory to just submit to you a quote for a new product within a day or two.

Pros:

1) Quality: Over the many years I have been involved in sourcing, Asian factories have improved their workmanship. Just make sure that your correspondence is completely clear and that you have good working prototypes with easy-to-understand specifications. The old saying goes, "less is more," but in this case that most definitely does

NOT apply. Never worry that you are sending TOO MUCH information. The more accurate data you can furnish to the prospective supplier in Asia, the better the quality of your product will be.

2) Attitude: Most Asian suppliers are very interested in establishing a good business relationship with you. They will be eager to please you with the hope that you will continue to work with them for reorders once your product has become successful!

3) New jobs? Many worry that if they source their inventions in Asia, it will take away from jobs in the USA. This is not necessarily true.

Sourcing and manufacturing products in Asia in turn opens up numerous business opportunities here at home in logistics, distribution, computer graphics, sales and marketing. For example, dockworkers will need to unload your shipment off the vessel and send it by truck or rail to your warehouse, storage facility or distribution center. Your graphic artist will design your logo, labeling and packaging. And don't forget about the U.S. marketing firm that could get you some good PR. Once your product(s) are selling, reliable domestic trucking firms can make deliveries to retail outlets all over the USA!

4) <u>PRICING, PRICING, PRICING</u>! Did I say, "pricing?" Many new products can be sourced in China, depending on the industry, for anywhere from 1/2 to 1/8 of what it would cost to be manufactured in the USA. This is an obvious advantage to new business start-ups!

For many, the thought of manufacturing overseas is daunting, but with the proper guidance and reliable contacts it can be an option you may want to consider. As with any business plan, there are pros and cons that must be weighed. Remember, asking the right questions and understanding the answers is essential to success in any endeavor. Make sure the lines of communication are clear and you could find the cost savings of manufacturing overseas gives you enough breathing room to launch a successful product and grow a profitable business.

Inventor Story:

Should I Outsource?

Joe Yao, MD is an orthopedic surgeon who himself suffers from hand pain and numbness while driving a car or working on the computer. From his medical practice, Yao knew that he was not alone with this pain.

Several years ago, Yao's hands went numb while driving on the Interstate and he decided that he needed to come up with a solution. Numbness is caused by vibrations on the major hand nerves and most driving gloves have pads placed over these nerves, which transfer the vibration directly to the nerves. Yao thought that he could place pads around these nerves so that the vibration would be diverted away from the nerves, thereby reducing or eliminating numbness.

Yao did his market research, created a prototype and found that his product would need to sell for $17.50 to be competitive. When he started contacting glove manufacturers in the U.S., most were simply not interested. Of all the manufacturers he contacted, only two seemed interested. After receiving the schematics and a video explaining construction of the glove, the manufacturers were still hesitant to offer a quote. Yao kept on prodding the manufacturers to give him a quote. Finally one responded; $32 without shipping. For a product that retails at $17.50, that is clearly a non-starter. Manufacturing costs need to be 20-25% of the retail price.

When he started contacting glove manufacturers in the U.S. most were simply not interested.

At this point Yao realized that he would need to outsource manufacturing. He started by contacting international trade consultant, Edith Tolchin, of EGT Global Trading, and together they started corresponding with Chinese manufacturers for quotes. While Yao could only find two U.S. manufacturers even interested in looking at his product and only one who was willing to give a quote, he found the Chinese manufacturers had a much better attitude about gaining new business. Not all of the manufacturers responded, and some responded with very limited English, but the others responded promptly in reasonable English.

> **Yao found the Chinese manufacturers had a much better attitude about gaining new business.**

Yao's current manufacturer is very eager to help and do the job correctly. They do their best to work out any problems promptly with Yao and stand behind their product 100%. Their attitude shows they are thankful for the business and are doing their best not to lose it – the ideal attitude for your business associates to have.

Of course, outsourcing manufacturing hasn't been all easy for Yao. His product, Qwi™ Nerve Protection Gloves, http://www.qwinerveprotector.com/, is primarily sold to motorcyclists and truck drivers who tend to be very patriotic. Some potential customers refuse to buy the product simply because it is manufactured overseas. Sometimes explaining that U.S. manufacturers were unwilling to produce the product helps, but not always.

Yao also has had to be patient as he makes product changes. Originally he thought that truck drivers would be the best market, but he soon found out that it was a hard market to crack and he had to switch gears to focus on motorcyclists. This required a change in the product, which would have taken one or two days if manufacturing were based in the U.S., but it took months working with an overseas manufacturer.

> **A required product change, which would have taken one or two days if manufacturing were based in the U.S., took months while working with an overseas manufacturer.**

A constant challenge is projecting sales because it takes so long to receive a product shipment. Yao needs to order at least three months in advance so he doesn't run out of inventory, but a misjudgment can cause a shortage of one product and a surplus of another.

A misjudgment in sales projections can cause a shortage of one product and a surplus of another.

Yao has also had a string of quality issues, which actually forced him to change manufacturers. Even the new manufacturer has had problems with dye transferring from the gloves to the wearer's skin.

Despite these drawbacks, Yao has been happy with his choice of manufacturing overseas. His business is still in the early stages and success is by no means guaranteed, but he would never have gotten this far without outsourcing. Now Yao is honing his sales strategy and gaining a growing number of very satisfied customers who love the product so much that they tell all their friends about it.

Yao's business is still in the early stages and success is by no means guaranteed, but he would have never gotten this far without outsourcing.

Chapter 2

Are you ready?

You have worked long hours on developing your idea! Attorneys, prototypes, attempts at licensing, and it seems as though you are still just beginning! How do you finally get your product "out there?" A guest speaker at your monthly inventors' group meeting suggests that you might want to attempt a small production run, on your own, in China. Now what???

This chapter will address the some issues you should NOT overlook when sourcing and producing your invention in China.

Product Design Evaluation with an independent testing/safety lab: Yes, you believe your product is safe, but does it conform to the various regulations for imported products? There are so many US government agencies that oversee imported products, and each of those agencies has its own rules to follow; doing this research on your own can cause a whirlwind in your brain! You've got the Federal Trade Commission (www.ftc.gov), the Consumer Product Safety Commission (www.cpsc.gov), US Customs and Border Protection (www.cbp.gov) and many more. How do you make sure your invention meets these various standards? The CPSC has a list of independent testing/safety labs listed on their website. Contact several (there are many) and ask if they specialize in evaluations of new inventions. If so, then describe your invention to them (i.e., electronic, plastics, textiles, toy, etc.), and ask them for a price quote on having a Product Design Evaluation done.

"Why," you ask, do you need to work with an independent testing/safety lab? "My invention is perfectly safe!" It sure looks like that to the average consumer. But these labs are trained to look for issues that you or I would never ever think about. Use the example of a new type of children's plastic craft scissors, with rounded (safety) tips, etc. Seems safe enough right? Not to the safety/testing labs! What type of plastic is used? Are there any hazardous, environmentally unfriendly chemicals used in the components? Are there any parts that can come loose and pose a choking hazard? Has it been "age-graded" so that (for example) if you intend for it to be used by children ages 3 and older, what happens if 15 month-old little sister Susie grabs hold of them and bites off the handle!?!?!?! Has it been properly marked to show country of origin (as required by US Customs and Border Protection's regulations)? The list goes on and on.

A Design Evaluation is my favorite tool for beginning the product development of your invention. The labs will thoroughly review your product for any "red flags" or possible safety issues and provide a list of recommended modifications to get your product into compliance. They will also address the numerous labeling, packaging and other government regulations for imported merchandise, all to be outlined in your report. The last part of the evaluation will be a thorough list of recommended production testing that should be done in one of their satellite offices in China, once your order has been placed with the China supplier. Although the headquarters for most of these labs may be located in the USA, most labs have satellite offices in many cities throughout China, which will frequently be very close to the factory where your order is being produced. It is advantageous to have the tests done in the China affiliate offices rather than at the US headquarters because the costs for production testing are frequently less expensive in China than in the lab's USA offices. There is also less transit time and shipping expenses involved in sending the samples for testing to another office within China rather than back to the USA.

With report in hand, you now know the modifications which must be done to your prototype, and are armed with production testing information to bring your invention into compliance with the various US government agencies' seemingly infinite requirements. This also helps with Product Liability Insurance, which every new business selling consumer products should have. And, your goal with proper production testing and addressing all safety issues is to make sure your new product NEVER appears on the Consumer Product Safety Commission's Product Recall List! (go to http://www.cpsc.gov/cpscpub/prerel/prerel.html). A Product Recall can make or break any new business!

Before you start the sourcing process and safety testing, make sure your product is right for your intended market. If you rush into manufacturing your product only to find out that the market is looking for a different product (much like Joe Yao did, as mentioned in Chapter 1), you may need to make substantial changes to your product's design. These changes may raise new safety issues, forcing your product to be evaluated by a testing lab again. You will save time and money if you get it right the first time so make sure you have done your market research.

If you are having a hard time discerning what exactly your intended market is looking for, consider hiring professional help. www.DonDebelak.com does low cost product evaluations that help you understand your target market and how to develop your product so it best meets the needs and desires of those potential customers. These evaluations by DonDebelak.com also offer help on distribution, competition and a myriad of other factors that can impact your product's chances for success.

"Perfected" prototype: You have heard that all you need to begin the sourcing process are detailed drawings or sketches of your product? Sometimes yes, but frequently NO! It is always better to have a *perfect* prototype to send to China. You have obtained your Design Evaluation from the safety/testing lab, so why on earth, after doing the ground work, would you send just the drawings? If you do, you will spend much time and energy on back-and-forth e-mails, attempting to convey the intricate details of your product, which unfortunately a sketch just cannot address. With China sourcing, what you see is what you get. So, even if you send over a rough prototype, it will take you many long e-mails trying to explain the modifications you want done, before placing an order. You will frequently encounter communication difficulties, as mentioned before. Yes, you most certainly can hire a translator to list all of the modifications in Chinese. This is what I would consider a good back-up plan, though it can be expensive. But the easiest, quickest and most efficient method for a pleasant sourcing experience is to have a perfect prototype done in the USA. There are many capable prototype specialists in all commodities, and many can be found at the website for the United Inventors Association (www.uiausa.org). USA prototype costs may be expensive, but will save you money in the long run, thus avoiding the costly Fedex charges for numerous back-and-forth submissions to and from China until they get it right, not to mention possible delays in launching your product, before your prototype is exactly as you want it.

Inventor Story:

Can my product be produced in China?

Karen Nadler-Sachs was feeding her two and a half year-old breakfast early one morning. To protect the upholstered dining room chair her daughter was sitting on, Nadler-Sachs placed a towel on the seat of the chair. After some squirming, the towel no longer completely covered the chair and a gob of jam fell directly on the exposed upholstery. At that time, Nadler-Sachs decided to invent something to protect her chairs and save her the trouble of constantly cleaning them.

Nadler-Sachs started sewing dozens of prototypes out of a variety of materials to try to get her design right. Once she had a good prototype, she took it everywhere with her – to her friends' houses, to furniture stores – to make sure it would fit on all types of chairs. Then she worked with prototypers and design engineers to perfect the final design.

At this point, Nadler-Sachs started investigating manufacturing. She quickly realized that U.S. manufacturers were not able to produce her product at a price that would make it competitive and allow her to make a profit. She set her sights overseas, but she had a big problem: she only wanted to make a small production run to test the waters.

Nadler-Sachs decided that she needed some help and contacted international trade consultant Edith Tolchin. Tolchin knew a few manufacturers that would handle low volume production and set up production at one of those plants.

Nadler-Sachs submitted them a perfect prototype, which she spent lots of time working out with her prototypers, design engineers and even with the advice of a few friends. She knew what goes in comes out, so a stitch in the wrong place will be replicated on every single product.

Once the samples came back, Nadler-Sachs poured over every seam and every letter of the label to make sure it was all perfect. Then she ordered her first 1,000 units of product, which is named, "Save the Chairs!" http://www.savethechairs.com.

Although Nadler-Sachs only wanted 1,000 units, she was able to manufacture in China to give her product a test run in the U.S. She did her homework and made sure her prototype was perfect so that her end product was perfect.

<u>Chapter 3</u>

How to Find a China Factory on Your Own

Finding a good, reliable Chinese manufacturer can be intimidating for a first time inventor. Listed below is everything you need to know to find a good manufacturer, but many inventors still look for help to import their first product. An international trade consultant will know all of the ins and outs of locating and working with an overseas manufacturer.

<u>Creating a List of Potential Manufacturers:</u> To find a good manufacturer, go to one or all of the websites listed on the right.

- **www.alibaba.com**
- **www.chinasources.com – (www.globalsources.com)**
- **www.ttnet.net**
- **www.tradeeasy.com**
- **www.sourcingcreator.com**

Start by entering the type of product you want manufactured and the country from where you want to purchase it. This can difficult for new inventions if they create a new product category, since the existing search options will not help you. So, you should find a general category that your invention may fit into – for example, hats, radios, toys, tablecloths, brooms, and so on.

That should help you locate manufacturers of products similar to your invention.

Another way to develop a list of potential manufacturers is to network with other inventors who have inventions similar to yours. If they have manufactured overseas, ask about their experience with their manufacturer.

Making Initial Contact: After you have created a good list of potential manufacturers, contact them and ask for references of American firms with whom they have worked with. If they are concerned with confidentiality, ask for some brand names they manufacture, that you might recognize in US stores.

When they respond, assess their ease in communication, their mastery of the English language, and their promptness in replying. If they take a week to reply to an initial e-mail, that will usually be an indication that they will not be very good at getting back to you, and this could delay the development of your product.

Many Asian suppliers will claim (sometimes for their convenience – they can't be bothered, they're too busy) that they do not want to violate confidentiality. But if they are working with big USA companies

(Walmart, Home Depot, etc.), then you most definitely want to know this! This is a good thing. A sign of a capable, confident source is if they volunteer the names of recognizable USA companies they have manufactured for. Besides, just by giving a business partner's name, it does not reveal any product details.

If they do not want to give you the names of USA buyers, then be persistent and ask them for some USA brand names (i.e., Disney, Liz Claiborne, America's Pride) of products that you might recognize in retail shops. This obviously does not create a confidentiality issue because the products are already out there!

If they cannot give you either references and/or USA brand names, don't waste your time dealing with them. Go with someone who has a proven track record.

Upon receiving a list of references, contact them and ask how their experience was with the manufacturer. If other companies have had bad experiences, chances are you will too.

Asking for Quotes: After contacting the references that the manufacturers have provided, hopefully you will have narrowed down your list to at least five good prospects. Put together a package to send to each of those manufacturers that includes samples of your prototype, along with all product literature, specifications, measurements, components, etc. Many sources can work with drawings, but it is more efficient to use actual prototypes, as mentioned in Chapter 2. Also include any safety issues you will want addressed, taken from your Design Evaluation report from the independent testing / safety lab, and any production tests that they must comply with, also from the Design Evaluation.

Make sure to include an introduction letter, indicating the quantity you are looking to buy, the ports into which you would like to ship your order, and any special features of your product that need to be included, which might not be obvious to the supplier when they first look at your prototype.

Give as much info as possible – communication can be difficult and the more information you give the more likely your product will turn out right.

Finding an International Trade Consultant: If at this point you are feeling overwhelmed, you may want to hire an international trade consultant. To find one, read the classified ads in Inventors' Digest magazine, whether via hard copy or online at www.inventorsdigest.com. Look under their Classifieds. You can also contact the United Inventors Association:

www.uiausa.org, or look under "Professional Member Listings" at the website.

There are also a few important trade organizations to consider: First, the Federation of International Trade Associations (www.fita.org) is a good place to start. And, you may contact the National Customs Brokers & Forwarders Association of America, Inc. at: www.ncbfaa.org. Although you may not need a Customs Broker or Freight Forwarder immediately, many customs brokerage firms employ international trade consultants or may be able to recommend one.

Last, if your invention is a textile or sewn item, bag, baby accessory, arts & crafts product, small household invention or fashion item, you may contact me, Edie Tolchin, at EGT@warwick.net.

Inventor Story:

Finding a Manufacturer

Brian Donnelly was an industrial design professor at San Francisco State University when he started designing his LifeSpan Furnishing product line. His first product was the Easy Up chair, a chair with longer arm rests and legs pointed outward to make it easy to get up out of the chair, but hard to knock it over in the process. The Easy Up had already won many awards for its senior-friendly design and he was ready to go into full production.

Donnelly started contacting U.S. manufacturers, trying to strike a licensing deal, but they all wanted too much money. He started to peruse furniture stores that would make something similar to his original design, which was made of metal. He found some products made by a Chinese manufacturer that were similar to what he envisioned for his product and learned that they were distributed by Iem, a company based out of California.

When Donnelly contacted Iem, they not only were willing to help him set up production, they wanted to invest in the product. Iem used its network to get the Easy Up chair into production. When Donnelly decided to expand his line to include wooden products, something that Iem and its network didn't do, Iem was able to use its contacts to find a reliable wood furniture manufacturer for Donnelly.

Since Donnelly started his business, he has found another way to locate manufacturers: industry trade shows. At all the international furniture fairs he attends, there are booths from Asian country trade councils looking for U.S. companies to manufacture their products in their home countries. These councils are willing to go the extra mile in getting you set up in their country, although you still need to be careful in taking the proper steps to determine if the factories themselves are reliable.

Inventor Story:

Finding a Representative

In 2003, Keith Wickenhauser owned a bar and grill. He noticed that people were constantly losing their keys, cell phones, cigarettes, and lighters – but no one ever lost their drink.

Wickenhauser thought that a product that could keep a drink and some small personal items together would be a great idea. Over the years, he had sold can coolers and given them away as promotions and he knew that the market was strong for such products, so he decided to take his idea and turn it into a promotional can cooler, the Wickooler, http://wickooler.com/.

After finishing developing the product, Wickenhauser had a U.S. manufacturer make some prototypes. He showed these to customers at convenience stores and had them rate the value of the product compared to other similar products. By doing this, he determined that $4.99 was the price that people would pay for his product.

After researching manufacturing costs in the U.S., Wickenhauser realized that he would need to take his product overseas to be manufactured. He did not feel comfortable is navigating the whole system himself, so he asked a friend who has experience in importing. His friend recommended a representative located in Asia that he had worked with in the past.

Wickenhauser has used this representative to locate a manufacturer, negotiate the price, oversee production schedules and handle quality control.

Chapter 4

Narrowing Down Your Choices and Negotiating with the 'Winning' Factory

After you have sent your five prototype samples and information to different factories, you should start receiving quotes in 2-4 weeks. The quotes may be similar or quite varied, but you don't want to choose a factory solely on price. There are issues of quality, promptness and reliability that can make or break your product and these issues simply cannot be overlooked. Below are some important questions to ask your potential manufacturers.

- **Can you provide recommendations of proposed alternate materials?**

- **Can you please give me a list of holidays when your factory will be closed for the current year?**
- **What is your delivery lead time?**
- **What policies do you have in place for replacement of defective merchandise?**
- **Do you work with a China freight forwarder who could arrange our shipment?**
- **What are your MOQs (minimum order quantities)?**
- **Are you willing to cooperate with the Asian affiliate of our appointed independent safety / testing lab?**
- **Do you work with a translator?**

1) **<u>Can you provide recommendations of proposed alternate materials</u>?** For example, your prototype is made of leather, but you are seeking a less expensive, but attractive alternative. Will they offer you samples of other fabrics (canvas, nylon, polyester)? This will help determine their eagerness to please and their problem-solving skills, which are very important with a foreign supplier.

2) **<u>Can you please give me a list of holidays when your factory will be closed for the current year</u>?** This is very important, because China

factories have many holidays where they are closed and therefore your production (and other product development stages) comes to a halt for as many as two to three weeks, especially during Chinese New Year, typically at the end of January / early February. This way, you can adjust your schedules accordingly.

3) **<u>What is your delivery lead time</u>?** In other words, from the time we approve both the pre-production and mass-production samples, how much longer will your factory require before my order is placed on a vessel (or air cargo)?

4) **<u>What policies do you have in place for replacement of defective merchandise</u>?** I normally write a stipulation in all my purchase orders that clearly spells out how the supplier will replace any defective items, beyond the typical industry standard, indicating that they (the seller) will be responsible for not only replacing the defective product, but also for arranging for the collection, and return shipment of those items as well.

5) **<u>Do you work with a China freight forwarder who could arrange our shipment</u>?** For many small initial

orders, it can be easier and more economical for the supplier to arrange for the ocean freight and marine insurance to be prepaid, and coordinated by their appointed freight forwarder at the port in China. Also, sometimes the factories get cheaper freight rates than if arranged in the USA. Your unit cost will increase by a few cents, but it will be worth not having to deal with steamship companies for quotes, making the arrangements with not-so-reliable trucking firms in China, inferior roads and transportation systems within China, and so on.

6) **<u>What are your MOQs (minimum order quantities)</u>?** This one is a biggie! If you are only in the position, as most start-ups are, to purchase a small number of pieces to begin with, you must state this up-front. Many Asian firms – especially the larger ones – will assume you are interested in purchasing their "typical" MOQs from the start. These "typical" MOQs can be upwards of 50,000 – 100,000 units! So, if you only want to buy 1,000 to "test the (market) waters," that should be the very first subject you discuss. You don't want to get too far along with prototypes, counter-

samples, and so on, only to lead the source on, thinking you will buy these huge quantities, and then he/she will quote you a price break, for 50,000 – 100,000 – 250,000 units! You can certainly volunteer that you will only be buying a small quantity to begin with, but if your product sells well, you will be back to them in the future for a quote for larger quantities.

7) **Are you willing to cooperate with the Asian affiliate of our appointed independent safety / testing lab?** The answer for this one should be obvious: if they say no, or are non-

committal, run for the hills. If your invention is an item with possible safety issues (for product liability insurance purposes), you will NEED to have production testing done. Your mission is to make sure your new product never appears on the Consumer Product Safety Commission's (www.cpsc.gov) Recall List. You can literally "lose you shirt" if this happens.

8) **Do you work with a translator?** You can almost always expect a small communication problem, which is why I recommend working with an international trade consultant

or another inventor who has imported from China before, because "Chinese-English" terms are frequently very different from "American-English" terms. Your supplier's command of the English language should be a very strong factor in your ease of building a business relationship. But if you find you are having too much difficulty, you can ask your prospective supplier to find a translator – or better yet, have the documents and/or specifications translated into Chinese BEFORE you send them. It may cost a couple hundred dollars, but it will save time and money in the long run.

At this point, you may have found that none of your potential manufacturers will work out. Don't worry, just put together another list of manufacturers and start again. There are thousands of factories in China so you still have plenty of options left. If you still have at least one potential manufacturer left, you need to make your final choice and start the negotiating process.

Your Chinese manufacturer will almost always expect you to negotiate on the final price of the product and shipping terms. Depending on your background and where you are from in the U.S., this may not be easy for you and you may want to enlist the help of someone who has some negotiating experience.

You can start the price negotiation process by simply sending a counter-bid. Keep it realistic, since if you really are interested in the prospective supplier, you do not want to be insulting.

Another way to open negotiations is to suggest your desired price in your introduction letter when you submit your prototypes. For example, you might write: "I am expecting to pay for 5,000 pieces. at US$2.50 per piece", which should normally be a few cents lower than what you'd expect to pay. This way, if the supplier counters with a bid of US$2.60 per piece, it may still be within your acceptable price range.

Most China factories quote payment / shipping terms either as "FOB China" pricing, which WILL NOT include ocean freight and marine insurance, or "CIF USA" port pricing, which WILL include freight and insurance. This is also negotiable. I typically prefer "CIF USA" port pricing because the supplier makes all the arrangements, frequently via their freight forwarder and steamship company in China, and issues a marine insurance policy as well. All you will have to do, when the shipment arrives in the USA, is have your (USA) customs broker clear your shipment for you, prepay import duties, and arrange transportation from the port to your inland delivery destination.

With “FOB China” pricing, however, you and/or your freight forwarder would have to make all arrangements to book space with a steamship company in China, obtain marine insurance, etc., all of which can be a bit more costly if arranged from the USA instead of in China. Your supplier would then just be responsible for shipping the cargo to the appointed vessel at the Chinese port, and the rest is your responsibility. There will be more on this in Chapter 5.

Also be aware of the payment terms. Typical payment terms are 30% down payment at time the purchase order is signed, sent via wire transfer from your bank to the China supplier's bank in China. The factory then goes into production, and all steps are taken as mentioned in Chapter 2, including pre-production sampling, production testing, quality control, mass-production samples, etc. When you, the buyer, approve the final mass-production samples, the supplier prepares the shipping documentation, which should be reviewed by either your international trade consultant or your customs broker, and arranges space on a vessel (or air cargo). The supplier will present you with proof of shipment and at that point you can arrange for the balance of 70% to be transferred from your bank to theirs.

With large volume orders, payment via Letter of Credit (L/C) can be used, but that is for merchandise worth (typically) hundreds of thousands of dollars. Letters of Credit can carry very steep bank fees for discrepancies in documentation, so that is why they are typically used only for larger purchase orders. There is almost always a discrepancy between L/C terms and shipping documents, which have to match up perfectly. Even so much as a misspelled word can cause an L/C discrepancy. As a first time importer, you definitely want to use bank wire transfers.

Inventor Story:

I Need a Good Manufacturer!

Many women match every outfit they wear with a handbag, but often they either don't have a coordinated wallet or they don't have time to move all of their cards, pictures and other things to their coordinated wallet. This frustrated Shannon Greenfield every time it happened to her. She remembers saying: "Someone should make a wallet that allows us to easily change the outer appearance of our wallet without removing the contents." And Shannon became that someone!

Greenfield made a variety of prototypes until she found something that really worked, and then she used the Thomas Register to find U.S. manufacturers. She wrote, emailed and called the leather manufacturers listed, but all to no avail. Either it was too costly, the manufacturers didn't have the resources, couldn't meet the timelines or they did not work with small projects. Greenfield had to take her product overseas.

She found an independent sourcing consultant, Edith Tolchin, and started contacting Chinese manufacturers. Greenfield was concerned about finding a reputable manufacturer and made sure to do a lot of shopping around to find one that could really meet her needs. Her product needed to have a sleek, fashionable look and poor workmanship would kill the business. She made sure to ask all of the questions listed in this chapter and didn't commit to a manufacturer until she got good answers so she would know that she had a flexible, reliable supplier creating her wallots™ -- www.wallots.com.

Inventor Story:

Can You Make My Product?

John Shoenhair of Strategic Solutions is a home martini maker. His brother-in-law was telling him about how to make the perfect martini and he realized that something was missing in the process to really make it easy. After spending a few months of product development, Shoenhair applied for a patent for his new martini glass.

Shoenhair spent about a year unsuccessfully trying to license the idea and decided to try to start selling the product on his own. He searched for U.S. manufacturers, but found no one did the high quality, hand blown crystal he needed. He used some companies that try to connect entrepreneurs with overseas manufacturers, but even then only one or two companies could be found, and they were much too expensive. Shoenhair decided to look on his own.

After searching on the internet, Shoenhair compiled a list of potential manufacturers and found one that responded quickly to his requests and offered reasonable quotes. The deal sealer was that they also had a good line of similar products that gave Shoenhair the confidence that they could deliver his martini glass at the quality he needed.

Chapter 5

Placing a Purchase Order, Payment and Shipping Terms

You've been corresponding with a factory in China who has sent you great counter-samples and who has even made some suggestions to improve your original prototype. You are ready to place an order, and will jot down a few items you require, such as quantity, price, etc. You will e-mail these items in an informal purchase order to your new supplier, and everything will be ok, right? Wrong!

For your protection (and that of your new start-up business venture), make sure a properly written purchase order is drawn up. This is a contract between you and the Chinese manufacturer. Include buyer / seller names and addresses, phone/fax numbers, e-mail addresses, quantities, unit pricing (determine in advance if you will be paying "FOB China" pricing, which WILL NOT include ocean freight and marine insurance, or "CIF USA" port pricing, which WILL include freight and insurance – see sidebar for the "13 Incoterms"), payment terms, shipping terms, mold / tooling charges, and wire transfer details such as percentage for down payments (usually 30% down). Also include your list of production testing (as determined in your Design Evaluation, as mentioned in Chapter 2), where it will be done, and who is paying for the tests. The most important item to incorporate into your PO is a STIPULATION FOR DEFECTIVE MERCHANDISE. Under a "comments" or "remarks" column in the POs I issue on behalf of my clients, I write, "Seller (name) is responsible for defective merchandise. Seller will be responsible for the entire cost of merchandise, freight charges for return of defective items, to be returned to the seller, in addition to replacement of the defective merchandise OR refund of buyer's payment (in U.S. dollars, at the option of the buyer, via Wire Transfer.)" Also provide all specifications, product description, components, Customs information (to be discussed in Chapter 6), labeling and production testing (both in accordance with your Design Evaluation report), packaging information, carton marks, and international shipping documentation requirements.

For purchase orders, the more info you provide, the more protection you hold, and your supplier will not be able to say, "Oops! You never mentioned that!"

An important set up of terms to know are called Incoterms 2000, which is a list of international rules for interpreting the most frequently used trade terms in international commerce. It consists of a series of 13 three-letter abbreviations.

The 13 Incoterms

Departure Terms

EXW – Ex-Works, lists the location where the shipment is available to the buyer, often location of the seller. Buyer assumes all responsibility for the product at pickup and arranges for all transportation.

Main Carriage Unpaid

FCA – Free Carrier: seller arranges and pays for transportation to the buyer's freight carrier, who then takes charge of the product at buyer's expense.

FAS – Free Alongside Ship: only for ocean shipments, the seller delivers shipment to the dock named by the buyer, after which the buyer arranges and pays for the remaining transportation.

FOB – Free On Board: only for ocean shipments, the seller delivers shipment to the dock and loads it onto the vessel named by the buyer, after which the buyer pays for the remaining transportation.

Main Carriage Paid

CFR – Cost and Freight, only for ocean shipments: the seller delivers shipment to the dock, loads it onto the vessel and prepays for shipping.

CIF – Cost, Insurance and Freight, only for ocean shipments: the seller delivers shipment to the dock, loads it onto the vessel, prepays for shipping and includes a marine insurance policy.

CPT – Carriage Paid To: the seller arranges and pays for shipment to a named destination.

CIP – Carriage and Insurance Paid To: the seller arranges and pays for shipment to a named destination and provides insurance for the shipment.

Arrival

DAF – Delivered At Frontier: for delivering to a land frontier, the seller arranges and pays for shipment to a named location, not unloaded and not cleared for import – meaning before the Customs border.

DES – Delivered Ex-Ship: only for ocean shipments, the seller arranges and pays for shipment to a named port, not unloaded and not cleared for import.

DEQ – Delivered Ex-Quay: only for ocean shipments, the seller arranges and pays for shipment to a named port, unloads the shipment onto the wharf, but does not clear the shipment for import.

DDU – Delivered Duty Unpaid: the seller arranges and pays for shipment to a named location, not unloaded and not cleared for import.

DDP – Delivered Duty Paid: the seller arranges and pays for shipment to a named location, not unloaded, but cleared for import.

The two most frequently used shipping terms when doing business with China are: "FOB" as in "FOB Shanghai", which means that the unit price being paid does NOT include ocean freight or marine insurance, which are to be arranged by the buyer via their freight forwarder or directly with the steamship company. "CIF", as in "CIF Miami", means that the unit price being paid to the China supplier will include COST, INSURANCE (usually marine insurance) AND FREIGHT (usually OCEAN freight), prepaid and arranged by the China supplier.

Payments

International purchase orders are usually paid by either Letter of Credit or wire transfer. As mentioned in Chapter 4, Letters of credit are used more often for larger quantity orders because of high fees and charges for discrepancies. The most widely used form of payment is a Wire Transfer, which means that money is transferred from your USA bank to the overseas supplier's bank. Typically a 30% down payment is placed by wire transfer to enable the supplier to purchase the raw materials necessary to begin production. After production is completed and all samples are approved (we'll get to quality control in Chapter 7), the 70% balance is paid by wire transfer ONLY after the supplier presents you with a copy of the ocean or air shipping document as proof of shipment.

Inventor Story:

The Importance of a Purchase Order

When Maureen Howard's first child was six months old, he was not napping well. Only if he was wrapped warm and tight would he sleep better. Howard wanted to create an easier way to keep her son warm and snug and she created a homemade prototype of her Magic Sleep Suit, www.magicsleepsuit.com, which worked so well that she decided to turn it into a product and sell it.

Howard realized that she couldn't afford to make her product in the U.S. and was referred to Edith Tolchin. They found a manufacturer in China and started getting ready for production, but then some problems arose and for about six months they lost the manufacturer.

Howard decided to reconnect with the manufacturer and see what happened. Once she found out the issues, they were able to come to a mutual agreement to move forward. Howard ended up paying more per unit, but it was worth the additional costs because the cost to change to a new manufacturer would have been much greater. Additionally, she had already lost valuable time, and did not want to start all over again.

Once the manufacturer and Howard were on the same page, they signed a revised Purchase Order to document the changes in their agreement. With this new PO, Howard was confident that the manufacturer would honor their side of the new agreement and if any problems arose, she had a legal document to fall back on.

Chapter 6

US Customs and Border Protection Issues

So, you have determined that offshore manufacturing is the best solution for bringing your invention to market, right? Able to stick to the tight "start-up" budget for your newly formed business because you have now seen that it is very frequently cheaper to make your product in another country? The quality of the counter-samples you have been receiving from the various prospective sources is excellent – just as good as, if not better than those you had received from domestic factories?

Excellent quality counter-samples, cheaper costs, the Internet, which brings the entire world to your fingertips – you've done your preliminary research! Now what? When the factories have completed production, independent testing labs have performed their magic, you and your international trade consultant have "dotted all I's and crossed all T's," and you are ready to have your first order shipped - HOW MUCH IN IMPORT DUTIES WILL YOU BE PAYING FOR YOUR INVENTION???

IMPORT DUTIES – What!? Why!? How!? Have you ever traveled abroad and made some neat purchases of gifts and goodies that you haven't, or couldn't have found at home? You know that, when you return to the USA from a foreign country, you will have to go through Customs (formerly U.S. Customs Service – now called, "Customs & Border Protection, div. of the U.S. Dept. of Homeland Security"). If you have purchased over a certain dollar value of these items (depending on which country you visited), they must be declared with the Customs inspectors, and you must pay duty on the amount in excess of the allowed merchandise value (keep receipts)! Did you think that when you import your great new invention into the shores of the good ole' USA it would be any different? YOU MUST STILL PAY DUTY ON THE

MAJORITY OF PRODUCTS IMPORTED INTO THE USA.

How do we find out how much duty you must pay on your soon-to-be imported invention? The two options are, first, to comb through the quite lengthy tome entitled the "Harmonized Tariff Schedule of the United States," published through the U.S. International Trade Commission. The "HTS" consists of two very detailed logs, the size of two Manhattan (NYC) phone books, with duty classifications for every product "under the sun", from animals, to fireworks, to raincoats, to computers parts! This guide can also be obtained online, but here's the catch: you must know what to look for! And, since the "HTS" shows duty classifications for "established" products, WHERE EXACTLY DO YOU CLASSIFY YOUR NEW INVENTION? Since most inventions are NEW ITEMS, chances are they won't be listed in the "HTS"! Sure, there may be a similar category – for example, you invented a special type of towel with unique pockets and other fabulous features. Do you look under Chapter 52-"Cotton" or under Chapter 63-"Other made up textile articles?" Good question, right? If you look into any of these chapters, there are so many different options – headings, subheadings, etc. - that after just a minute of reading through them, your brain begins to do a flashdance, out of synch, with your eyes! Again, since your product is unique – that's why it's called an invention – it is very difficult for a first-time importer to determine what the proper classification is for his/her product, in order to determine the duty amount to be added to their "landed" costs. What do you do next?

The old Greyhound commercial stated, "leave the driving to us!" Here is your second option: I recommend you ask your international trade consultant (I think every inexperienced prospective importer should work with one!) or licensed customs broker to prepare a request for a Customs ***Binding Ruling*** for your product. The Binding Ruling serves as protection for you, the importer. A sample (prototype is fine) of your invention, along with any literature you have available such as specification sheets, sales literature or brochures, packaging samples, labels, component information, etc., are sent to Customs, with a letter describing the ultimate use of your product, information about your company (to be called the “Importer of Record”), the manufacturer (if known at the time of ruling request), terms of sale, the ports through which you plan on importing the shipment(s) and any other information you or your representative feel may assist Customs in properly classifying your product.

WHY BOTHER? An example I always use is: your first shipment is due into port and is presented for customs clearance. Customs assigns a 5% duty rate and clears your shipment. You have paid 5% on the cost of your product. So, if the documentation shows that your product value was $10,000, the duty you paid was $500. About 6 months later, your invention has been very successful and this time you are importing a shipment valued at $100,000! You have budgeted the duties to now be $5000 (5%), right? WRONG! Without a Binding Ruling on a new invention with no other similar products listed in the "HTS," classifications (determination of import duties) are subject to interpretation by Customs at time of import. Another Customs Inspector who reads your shipment documentation this time may feel that the classification would carry an 8% duty rate. You are now paying $8000 even though you had budgeted only $5000 in duties! So, how do we avoid the "3 Gs" – (Gambling Guessing Game)??? Now you've got it right: A ***BINDING RULING***!

Why is this important? Improperly classified merchandise can carry very steep penalties! Your first shipment will take at least 45-60 days and US Customs will review the product and classify it within 30 days after receipt of sample. Since you have time anyway, you should take this very helpful precaution. Customs will even return your prototype if you wish, they will provide you with the duty rate, and even address international labeling and marking issues if you request this information. Proper labeling of your product and marking of your export cartons are also important to help avoid the possibility that your shipment may be detained for improper marking and/or labeling upon arrival in the USA. Penalties can be steep. Later on, when your shipment arrives in the USA, a copy of this Binding Ruling is presented during customs clearance. US Customs likes when you make it easy for them! So, to paraphrase another old saying, "it's not nice to fool Mother Customs!" Do it right from the very start, and you will have the satisfaction of knowing what you'll pay in import duties for all forthcoming shipments for your wildly successful "baby!"

Here are some important things to consider are if you want to employ a Customs broker and/or a freight forwarder. Freight forwarders are shipping companies who arrange your shipment, in the case of importing, typically from the overseas country into the USA, via air or ocean. Customs brokers are companies (or individuals) who hold US customs broker licenses. They are permitted to clear your shipment (whether via air or ocean) when it comes into the US Customs territory (i.e.

USA port), and thereby import the shipment on your behalf, with your signed Customs Power of Attorney form. They will prepay duties, prepare necessary documentation, and then deliver the shipment to your inland delivery destination.

If you have never imported before, it is wise to use a Customs Broker, who will guide you through all the steps necessary to legally import your shipment into the USA. You can obtain a recommendation via someone who has imported before, or you can contact the National Customs Brokers & Forwarders Association of America, Inc. at www.ncbfaa.org.

Inventor Story:

The News Might Be Bad, But At Least You'll Know

Maureen Howard (from Chapter 5), with the assistance of Edie Tolchin of EGT Global Trading, applied for a binding ruling for her Magic Sleep Suit. Her product is in a new category, so she didn't know what kind of import duties she would need to pay. It turns out that the duties were much higher than she expected, but now at least she knows and can plan for the expense by figuring it in to her final product price.

Chapter 7

Quality Issues, Safety and Production Testing and Product Liability Insurance

Every product should have product liability insurance, especially products manufactured in China. Take examples of recent Product Recalls from the (US) Consumer Product Safety Commission, www.cpsc.gov/cpscpub/prerel/prerel.html, for lead levels in children's toys from China. Independent safety testing is critical and should be done in conjunction with product liability insurance. Your insurance provider may give you some guidelines for product testing, but if not, it is far better to have your product safe from the start and go above and beyond to ensure your product is as safe as possible. If your product gets labeled as "unsafe", your image may be ruined forever, even if you make all the necessary changes to make the product safe.

Many large insurance companies provide business product liability insurance. A good product liability insurance provider is www.marshallandsterling.com.

Let's say that mass-production of your order is almost completed and your product has passed all of the production tests that were recommended in the Design Evaluation from the independent safety lab, as indicated in Chapter 2. The tests that you have chosen should have all been done at this point. Samples of production testing are: colorfastness, seam strength, shrinkage and toxicity in packaging. The tests should be done on a pre-determined number of actual mass-production samples to test for consistency in quality throughout the stages of manufacturing. You should have also approved all pre-production and mass-production samples, as part of the terms of your purchase order with the China factory. Your contact at the factory advises you that your order should be ready to ship in about

7-10 days. What should you do next? Order a *Final Shipment Inspection*!

Sure, the production samples that the factory sent you were good. And, they passed the safety tests. But how do you know that the shipment is consistent in quality throughout the numerous cartons, that it is packaged properly, and that your product has all of its components, labels, etc.? You need to have an inspection firm do a Final Shipment Inspection.

You should provide your desired inspection criteria for the firm's technician, including – if possible – photos showing "perfect" product vs. defective product, and even an actual sample of the product inside its packaging, with labels and all components. You may even give the technician a copy of the purchase order, which will clearly indicate shipping marks for cartons, labeling requirements, and so on.

A Final Shipment Inspection can be done by an inspection firm in China, such as KRT Audit Corporation, (www.chinainspect.com).

The technician schedules an appointment with the China factory, performs the inspection in accordance with your desired criteria, and AQL (Acceptance Quality Level) in accordance with the ISO (International Organization of Standards). In a very short time, you are provided with the Final Shipment Inspection report, which will be very thorough, and will include photos and comments on every aspect of your shipment. If there are any problems – and if you have allowed enough time – you may contact your supplier to make any necessary changes prior to shipment, either by e-mailing on your own, or by sending the technician's photos and/or even sending a copy of the Final Shipment Inspection report.

You can never be too safe with quality issues. Selling defective products will only do you harm; and, if you receive a shipment of bad products, even if your manufacturer is willing to replace entirely at its own cost, you will have lost valuable time and energy, either delaying the launch of your product or causing you to run out of inventory, thereby stalling sales efforts. Most retailers doubt inventors' ability to deliver products on time and consistently. Running out of inventory can cause you to lose hard earned retail accounts, so make sure everything is perfect before it leaves the factory.

Inventor Story:

Safety is a Number One Concern

Maureen Howard's (from Chapter 5) Magic Sleep Suit was a baby product in a new category; therefore there were no well defined safety standards. Because safety is vital for every product, and even more so for baby products, Howard wanted to take every precaution to ensure that when her product hit the shelves, there would be no safety concerns.

Howard, with the assistance of EGT Global Trading, found an international testing agency that first evaluated the safety of her design. They made suggestions to improve the product, which Howard incorporated into the final design. Then as the manufacturer was getting ready for production, she had the testing agency again test the pre-production samples to try to catch any other safety concerns.

While it is difficult to develop safety standards for a new product category, experienced testing agencies know what kind of red flags to look for and with their help, hopefully you will avoid a Product Recall from the CPSC.

Inventor Story:

What Kinds of Things Can Go Wrong?

Joe Yao, MD (from Chapter 1) has had some quality control problems with his Qwi^{TM} Nerve Protection Gloves, http://www.qwinerveprotector.com. He does not employ an independent testing agency, but his manufacturer does provide him with a final quality control report on every shipment, plus sends production samples. Yao has already caught some problems based on the production samples, like the nerve pads in the wrong location, but there are more subtle problems that he was not able to detect.

A couple of times the manufacturer has substituted materials with disastrous results. The worst part is that the substituted materials looked so similar that Yao did not notice and the problem was only discovered when customers complained that the gloves were falling apart.

Yao's manufacturer has replaced all of the defective merchandise, but selling poor quality products is never good for your image.

Chapter 8

You're Ready to Ship… Now What?

The Final Shipment Inspection went well. Your supplier is preparing the order for shipment. Your purchase order indicates whether it will be going via ocean or via air. If, for example, it will be a prepaid ocean shipment (or in this case the shipping terms are "CIF New York" – which includes **C**ost, **I**nsurance and **F**reight to the port of New York), then the factory makes the arrangements with their China freight forwarder for your order to be placed on a vessel (or on an airplane for air cargo shipment). Once all arrangements are made, the factory will then send you a copy of the shipping manifest, dock receipt or cargo receipt as proof of shipment. At that point, you would issue a wire transfer payment for any balance due the supplier, which is typically 70% of the order value (if you have already sent, for example, a 30% down payment via wire transfer when your order was first placed). Your supplier will give you an ETA (estimated time of arrival) into your designated USA port, and will forward all necessary shipping documents, again – as stipulated in your purchase order, on to you, or your USA customs broker directly. It will be up to you or your consultant to contact the customs broker to send a copy of the Binding Ruling (as previously mentioned in Chapter 6 – to determine import duties), so that the broker will properly classify your product, clear your shipment at your designated USA port, prepay any import duties, and ship it from the port to your warehouse or other inland delivery destination.

In the case of "FOB" (Free On Board) shipping terms, where you are responsible for the ocean freight and marine insurance, you can go to Customs & Border Protection's website (www.cbp.gov) for a list of Customs Brokers in the USA. (In this case, you must pay for ocean freight and marine insurance, instead of having these costs added to your unit cost from your

China supplier, and prepaid and arranged by them.)

Contact a few of these Customs Brokers and they will give you the names of some freight forwarders they work with in China. When your supplier gives you the total number of cartons, volume and weights for your upcoming shipment, (also make sure the commodity is properly described on the documentation, such as ‘shoes,’ ‘mugs,’ ‘baby toys,’ etc.), the freight forwarder in China can give you a quote on the ocean freight and marine insurance, and they can also coordinate the collection of your order from the China factory when it is ready to go.

As previously mentioned, however, it's frequently less expensive to book a purchase order with "CIF" shipping terms, where ocean freight and marine insurance are prepaid by the China factory, because they often receive cheaper freight rates when all of this is arranged within China. You can also contact the National Customs Brokers & Forwarders Association of America, Inc. (www.ncbfaa.org) for further assistance.

Your consultant or your customs broker should inspect the international shipping documentation provided by the supplier, such as the commercial invoice, packing list, bill of lading, Certificate of Inspection, Marine Insurance Certificate, etc. to make sure all proper Customs information is included, that the product is properly described, and quantities and costs are correct. Just as with your purchase order contract, it is always better to have more information than less in international shipping paperwork.

When your order reaches the USA port, your customs broker will clear your shipment through Customs on your behalf, prepay any import duties, and deliver it to your warehouse or other final delivery destination. This is where having a Customs Binding Ruling, as previously mentioned, helps to expedite the customs clearance process.

Once your shipment clears Customs, you will need to decide if you or your Customs Broker will pick up your freight at the port. Typically, Customs Brokers have connections with reasonably-priced trucking companies and if you decide to have your Broker arrange delivery to your warehouse, garage or directly to your customer, they will prepay the freight charges and add it to your final Customs Brokerage invoice. Or, if the shipment is small (i.e. a few cartons), you might want to arrange to pick up your shipment at the pier, when the Broker tells you it's ready and sends you a pick-up Delivery Order.

Chapter 9

China Sourcing Checklist

Below is a short checklist to be used as a quick reference to help make sure you haven't forgotten anything. This is a good list to review a few times during the sourcing process and it also will help you understand the flow and timing of all the steps you need to take.

1) **Sourcing**: Locating foreign sources, checking their references, obtaining product samples. Presenting your prototype(s) for production of first counter-sample and price quotation. Exploring the possibility of locating an overseas buying agent (not

applicable in all cases) who coordinates all transactions with the manufacturer, for a small commission (usually 2-4% of F.O.B. cost of item). Present prototype sample to U.S. Customs for "verbal decision"", or "Binding Ruling", on import duty/tariff rate, as well as for any special documentation requirements.

2) **Means of Financing the Import**: Upon determination of product cost, negotiation with vendor/agent regarding method of payment, i.e., wire transfer (the most widely used method), cash in advance (not a good idea), or letter of credit, usually used on large volume, high value orders. Locating

an international bank to establish a credit line (for letters of credit).

3) **Sales contract**: Usually, a "Purchase Order". The first purchase order with a new vendor should be reviewed by your attorney or international trade consultant, if at all possible. Then a "sample" PO should be e-mailed or faxed to vendor/agent for their comments and review. All details must be included, such as method of shipment (air or ocean), inspections, special documentation, and especially proposed delivery dates. (This is VERY IMPORTANT, since foreign deliveries are RARELY on schedule). Finalize PO, sign, e-mail and/or mail original to vendor.

4) **<u>Letter of Credit</u>**: (If applicable) After credit line is established with bank, application is completed (not signed) and faxed on to vendor/agent for comments, review. Once this is done, Letter of Credit can be opened. Again, as mentioned above, this is usually for POs of very high value. Typically, wire transfers are sufficient for first orders, as previously discussed.

5) **<u>Customs Brokerage/Power of Attorney</u>**: A customs broker is appointed who will handle the customs entry/clearance process of the import transaction. A "power of attorney" form is sent to you to enable you/your company to be the "Importer of Record," and gives the customs broker your

P.O.A. to clear your shipments. Single-entry or Continuous Import Bonds are determined at this stage, and your customs broker will arrange this for you.

6) **Production**: Goods are then produced in the factory. Weekly expediting details must be provided, which give you the production/delivery status of your product. Production samples are sent to importer for approval. At this point, towards the end of production, if you wish, you may request daily delivery progress updates. Production testing should be arranged, in accordance with the Design Evaluation (DE) you've had with your independent safety / testing lab, if applicable.

7) **Shipment**: When goods are ready, you must advise the vendor/agent the method of shipment you will use. Since you have plenty of time during the production process, you can research the most economical freight rates. Marine Insurance should be opened at this time, if applicable. All of this depends on the shipping terms of your PO, whether (for example) FOB China, or CIF USA port, as previously mentioned.

8) **Payment**: If "wire transfer", vendor must meet all documentation requirements, then wire transfer is effected. If Letter of Credit, vendor and agent now work together to make sure ALL DOCUMENTS are presented to their (foreign) bank in a timely

fashion (usually no later than 7-10 days). Photocopies of these documents are IMMEDIATELY faxed or e-mailed to you for your review. Foreign bank transmits documents to your bank for L/C negotiation. Bank notifies you of any discrepancies, which you must review. Your account is debited for the amount of the commercial invoice, and any applicable bank fees. YOU NOW OWN THE GOODS. Vendor then receives his payment from his bank. Original documents are then sent to you for:

9) **Customs Clearance**: Original shipping documents are sent to local customs broker (usually at the port where goods enter the U.S.), along with a letter of instructions,

indicating where goods are to be delivered, once cleared by Customs. You determine method of shipment of the goods from the pier (or airport if it is an air shipment). If you use your own truck, trucker must be given a delivery order. If you use the customs broker's truck, you must advise them where to send the goods from the port (i.e. to your warehouse, directly to a customer, etc.) Clearance/entry is effected and import duties are prepaid. Customs broker sends you an invoice for these charges.

Chapter 10

How to Protect Your Product Idea

Overview

As defined by U.S. law, trademarks, servicemarks, copyrights, and patents are "intellectual property." In contrast, a car is considered "personal property," and a house and its land are considered "real property." For real property and personal property, what is owned can be seen and touched. What is owned as intellectual property can only be defined by words.

The Benefit of Patents

Inventors frequently ask Don Debelak, "how important is a patent?" His stock answer is that its importance is totally dependent on the value placed on a patent by the person with whom you are dealing. Don Debelak's experience is that in China, the manufacturers you deal with consider a patent important and place a high value on it. One can argue about whether a patent is weak or strong, but the fact is most people, especially overseas, expect you to have a patent and not having one can work against you. Whether the patent is strong or weak may be argued in the US, but overseas, people don't seem to try and evaluate if claims are broad or weak. What does count is having a patent.

Patent Searches

A "search" means looking at patents, magazines, product brochures, newspapers, and any written publication for information about what has already been thought of in the area or field of your **product**. When these written publications are found, they are called the "prior art." Prior art can be in a foreign language, and it doesn't have to be found in the United States or be easily available. Anything that is found may preclude getting a patent, and there is no differing level of importance among types of prior art; a magazine article can be just as meaningful as a prior patent. Inventors should realize that prior art that is searched will be less than half of the worldwide prior art, and that the U.S. patent examiner will see less than half of the worldwide prior art. That means that any patent issued by the USPTO may be found invalid later if better prior art is found, or if a company looking to copy your product can find previously unfound prior art.

Types of Patents

Utility Patents: The patent that gives the longest protection and is the most common patent inventors receive.

Definition: Utility patents cover new methods of doing something, new devices for doing something, and new chemical compositions. A method of advertising, a method of washing clothes, and a method of making a product can be patented—as can a device that holds advertising, a device that washes clothes, a machine for making a product, and equipment for producing a paint remover.

Requirements: The product must be novel (new) and unobvious (a new combination that a person skilled in the field would not have thought of). For example, a Post-It note has an adhesive that sticks to the note but easily peels off from the next note in the stack of Post-Its. The paper for the Post-It note is specially designed to do this, and that paper formula would not be obvious because that feature had never been seen before.

Advantages/Disadvantages: The main advantage is that you have an intellectual property right that can be enforced to stop your competitors from copying your method or device and which can be licensed or sold to others. Many companies that license products require you to have a utility patent. A patent also offers benefits in the marketplace, as people in the distribution channel and end users tend to perceive patented products as having more value. Some disadvantages are that a patent may not prevent competition, it is expensive, and there is no one to enforce a patent except the patent holder. Stealing an idea is a subject for civil courts and not criminal prosecution.

Design Patents: Design patents offer a low cost, but with correspondingly low protection approach to getting a patent

Definition: The design of an object—its shape or ornamental look—can be patented. Some examples are a car fender, a soap holder, and computer housing, such as the design of Apple's iMac computer.

Requirements: The design must be different from what has previously been done (as established by prior art). This can be a very arbitrary decision, but almost all design patents are approved.

Advantages/Disadvantages: The main advantage is that you now have an intellectual property right that you can enforce, license or sell. You can place "patent pending" on the product as soon as your application is accepted, and you no longer need to have confidentiality agreements signed. The main disadvantage is that any minor changes in what is shown in the drawings of your patent may be enough to allow the competition to design around your patent.

Provisional Patents: Buys you one year of time before you submit your formal patent; also gives you foreign patent rights.

Definition: Provisional patent applications are never examined, meaning that no one reads them, and they allow you one year to submit a regular utility patent. The provisional patent was originally created to protect U.S. inventors' foreign patent rights. U.S. patent law gives you one year to apply for a patent after you start selling your idea, while foreign patent law requires that you obtain a patent before any sales efforts or any publicity is released. Cost varies depending on the complexity of your idea.

Requirements: The application must explain in words and drawings everything about your product. Photographs can be photocopied onto paper and included; however, a drawing of what is shown in the photograph should be provided. The application will be examined when you submit your official utility patent to make sure they are the same, and then the filing date of the provisional application will be used if there is a future patent dispute or if the patent office needs to decide whom to give a patent to when two similar patents have been filed.

Advantages/Disadvantages: One main advantage is that you can do the provisional application yourself, and it is a very low cost alternative to a regular application. It is considered a reduction to practice because, similar to making a prototype, you have proved the product will work; you no longer need to use confidentiality agreements; and you can place "patent pending" on the product or method. It is a useful tool even if you never intend to apply for a utility patent, as it offers patent pending status for one year, and this should allow you enough time to evaluate the commercial potential of your product. The main disadvantage is that you are required to file a utility patent application within 12 months or forfeit your ability to patent the idea.

Other Tactics

Confidentiality Agreements and Nondisclosure Statements

Definition: This agreement goes by many names, but it is an agreement between you and another party (or person) not to disclose to a third party what you have shown them concerning your product.

Requirements: Some type of signed written statement where the person receiving confidential information agrees not to disclose the information to others.

Advantages/Disadvantages: The main advantage is that a confidentiality agreement makes the information you share with the other party a nonpublic disclosure under U.S. patent law, which in many cases protects your patent rights. Using such an agreement shows a very careful and businesslike approach to your dealings. The biggest disadvantage is that the agreement can't be enforced against a third party who learns from the signing party of your idea. Further, enforcement of the agreement against the signing party requires the filing of a lawsuit.

Inventor's Notebook

Definition: This is simply any kind of bound notebook—preferably one with numbered pages. If the pages are not numbered, number them yourself; this is done to show that no new pages were inserted at a later date. The engineering notebooks or accountants' ledgers sold in office supply stores are ideal.

Requirements: This should contain evidence of your activity—everything that you do should be entered into the notebook, in sequence, and dated. This includes drawings, ideas that you consider, and discussions with vendors and customers, along with the date and time of each event and notes on whether the interaction was in person or on the telephone. It should have a dated signature of one and preferably two people on each page with the notation, "The above material is confidential, and I have read and understood this page." Note: Have witnesses sign the book at least every week.

Advantages/Disadvantages: The main advantage is that it documents your product's progress and can be useful with potential partners and investors. It can also be useful in case you need to demonstrate the date that you first conceived your product and to show that the idea is indeed yours and that you didn't take it from someone else. The notebook can be easily kept up to date.

Patent Strategies

Don't Bother

Explanation: If you don't need a patent to sell a product, you might want to avoid the expense if you are selling to a small market or if your product can't support a broad patent claim.

Advantages/Disadvantages: Basically, it costs nothing to do nothing, but you can't prevent competitors. Products without patents are probably impossible to license.

Patent Pending Strategy

Explanation: Once you have applied for a provisional, utility, or design patent, you can place "patent pending" on your product. The patent pending notice will scare away most companies from copying your product. One way to use this strategy is to apply for a low-cost design patent or a provisional patent without any intention of filing a final patent. On short-term promotional items, or fad items with a short life span, the patent pending status might be all the protection an entrepreneur needs.

Advantages/Disadvantages: There are a number of advantages: Many competitors will not try to introduce a competitive product to one that is patent pending. Patent pending status is a better negotiating tool while getting a license, as the company won't initially know what your claims are.

Patent pending status is almost as useful as an awarded patent when introducing a new product, and patent pending status can last for as long as 20 years if you keep changing your product's design. The main disadvantage: It doesn't provide any real protection for your product.

Low-Quality Patents

Explanation: Design patents and utility patents with narrow claims don't offer significant barriers to competitors, but they still have a deterrent value for some competitors, still offer a marketing advantage, and still help entrepreneurs license their ideas. Since the patent will have limited real protection, entrepreneurs can save money by patenting the product themselves. Patent It Yourself (Nolo Press) by David Pressman is an excellent resource for this. You can also proceed with a patent attorney.

Advantages/Disadvantages: A low-quality patent allows you to have the marketing and psychological advantages of having a patent, but it doesn't offer significant intellectual property barriers to competition.

Broad Patent with Few Specifics or Limitations

Explanation: A utility patent with a broad claim is worthwhile, and you should use a patent agent or attorney to file the application for you. This claim will help prevent competition and leave you in the best position possible to license your idea.

Advantages/Disadvantages: A broad patent offers strong protection from competitors and offers entrepreneurs a better chance of landing a licensing arrangement. The disadvantages are mainly monetary. As you proceed with the patent process, you may have numerous objections and rejections from the USPTO. It can easily cost $1,000 to $2,000 for each response to the patent office. You can end up spending well over $20,000—and in the end your final claim might be much more narrow than you expected, giving you nothing like the protection you had hoped for.

Many Weak Claims

Explanation: Sometimes products have close prior art that limits the scope of a patent. However, that prior art may not compete with the entrepreneur's product, nor may it diminish the novelty of the product to the marketplace. One solution to this problem is to file as many specific claims as possible in an effort to tie up every possible design. When done correctly, this tactic, in effect, gives the product a broad patent. This will require the filing of many applications and the costly prosecution of each application to issue.

Advantages/Disadvantages: This strategy can provide broad patent coverage for items unique to the market that have narrow patent claims due to prior art. A large number of patent claims discourages competitors and also provides a perceived edge in marketing the product. The disadvantage, again, is that it is an expensive process.

Foreign Patents

Filing for a U.S. patent only protects you in the United States. To protect yourself elsewhere, you have to file foreign patent applications. The "patent cooperation treaty" (PCT) application can be used to file your product in foreign countries that have signed the treaty.

The advantage of the PCT application is that you can file the same patent application in many countries. The disadvantage is that your patent rights can be 10 times more expensive than filing only in the United States. The total expense can be over $100,000 if you patent your product in the major countries of Europe and Japan. The violators of your patent rights will be more expensive to find. And the patent system and the courts that enforce the laws in foreign countries may favor their own citizens and companies over U.S. entrepreneurs.

Recommended Books

- The Copyright Handbook (Nolo Press) by Stephen Fishman
- License Your Invention (Nolo Press) by Richard Stim
- Patent, Copyright and Trademark (Nolo Press) by Stephen Elias
- Patent Searching Made Easy (Nolo Press) by David Hitchcock
- Patent It Yourself, 7th edition (Nolo Press) by David Pressman
- Trademark: Legal Care for Your Business & Product Name (Nolo Press) by Kate McGrath and Stephen Elias with Sarah Shena

Infringement Remedies

When a person or a company uses your trademark or service mark on their products or services or makes, sells or uses your patented device or method, the only option to stop them provided by law is to sue them. The cost of a lawsuit is very high, and usually both sides understand this. Many times, all that you—or your attorney—need to do is to write a letter to the offending party explaining the possible violation of your intellectual property right. Your letter should be phrased that there is a possibility the product or the method infringes the claims in your patent and that you would like to discuss the issue with them.

US Patent Considerations when Outsourcing to China

A U.S. patent protects you rights only in the U.S. One of the risks of outsourcing to China is that your manufacturer or another manufacturer might knock off your product. If that happens, what can you do? Patent law allows you to sue anyone who illegally violates your patent rights. That means you can sue a consumer, a distributor, a retailer, or even the manufacturer itself. Suing the consumers isn't practical or cost effective and you won't have much luck trying to sue the Chinese manufacturer in China, so you have to go after every retailer and/or distributor selling the knock-off. Sometimes a letter will have the retailer stop selling the knock-off, but that doesn't mean they will buy yours at a higher price. Unless you have established a market, preventing the knock-off from being sold doesn't really help you. Even worse, sometimes nobody stops selling the product and you have to go out and sue everyone, which will cost you a small fortune and you are by no means guaranteed a victory in court

Acknowledgements

The vast majority of the information in this appendix was provided by Albert W. Davis, davis_al@msn.com, and Don Flickinger of Phoenix. Al Davis is a retired patent agent who has worked both independently with inventors and as an examiner with the U.S.

Patent Office. Don Flickinger has worked for nearly 40 years as a patent agent. Both are found in the list of registered patent agents found at www.uspto.gov.

Inventor Story:

What Can You Do if Your Patent Doesn't Protect You?

In the late 90's, Steve Vetorino had an idea for a new flashlight, charged not by batteries, but by magnetic force from shaking the flashlight. He teamed up with Jim Platt and Todd Brown to bring the product to market. By 1998, their NightStar flashlight was being sold through catalogs and sales were steadily growing.

By 2001, a Chinese manufacturer created a knock-off that was selling for $15 less than the NightStar. Soon retailers and catalogs were dumping the NightStar in favor of the lower priced knock-off. Up until that time, the NightStar had been manufactured in Denver, but Vetorino, Platt and Brown realized that now they needed to move their manufacturing overseas so they could continue to compete.

They found a good Chinese manufacturer that produced high quality products and they started to implement some product changes. Since Vetorino, Platt and Brown had been selling the product for a few years, they had some ideas on how to improve it that they hadn't had the time, or the necessity, to implement. They realized that they couldn't compete on price alone, but if they had a reasonable price, they could compete on quality.

They took their beefed up product to a number of testing agencies for certification to work safely in a number of dangerous environments. They got all of these certifications which mean that their flashlight is purchased by organizations like the U.S. military, mining companies, and others who are concerned about safety.

Vetorino, Platt and Brown have used their certification as their marketing edge, aggressively attacking small markets where quality counts. There have been more than ten other knock-offs to enter the market and still the NightStar's sales continue to grow.

Vetorino has a patent, but that hasn't stopped competitors from entering the market. His patent isn't very strong, so Chinese manufacturers have found ways to design their products around his patent. Regardless, Vetorino, Platt and Brown have been able to stay one step ahead of the competition and continue to increase their sales every year. When standard intellectual property protection doesn't work, you need to use business savvy to stay ahead of the game.

Chapter 11

Helpful Links

1) Harmonized Tariff System of the United States- (for information on classifying your product for import duties): http://www.usitc.gov/tata/hts/bychapter/index.htm

2) U.S. Customs and Border Protection- (for information on importing into the United States): www.cbp.gov

3) Consumer Product Safety Commission: www.cpsc.gov

4) Consumer Product Safety Commission's suggested independent safety / testing labs' link:

http://www.cpsc.gov/businfo/testtoylabs.html (although it says "toys," it does state that they handle "other products").

5) Consumer Product Safety Commission's Recalls and Product Safety News: http://cpsc.gov/cpscpub/prerel/prerel.html

5) Federal Trade Commission- (for information about labeling your products): www.ftc.gov

6) Federation of International Trade Associations: www.fita.org

7) National Customs Brokers & Forwarders Association of America, Inc.: www.ncbfaa.org

8) KRT Audit Corporation- (for shipment inspections): www.chinainspect.com

9) Pantone- (for international color standards): www.pantone.com

10) Inventors Digest Magazine: www.inventorsdigest.com

11) United Inventors Association: www.uiausa.org

12) Ask The Inventors: www.asktheinventors.com

13) INPEX- (America's largest invention trade show): www.inpex.com - typically held once a year, in June, in Pittsburgh, PA.

14) Yankee Invention Expo: www.yankeeinventionexpo.org – typically held once a year, in October, in Waterbury, CT.

15) For shipping terms info: Incoterms 2000: http://www.uscib.org/index.asp?documentID=2213

ADDENDUM

Under "Helpful Links"

CHAPTER 11, page 164

Please add:

16) INVENTOR MENTOR -

JACK LANDER

www.inventor-mentor.com

17) PROTOSEW -

BARRY HEIM

www.protosew.com

Thank you!

Afterword

CONGRATULATIONS!

YOU ARE NOW OFFICIALLY AN INTERNATIONAL TRADER!

Please bear in mind that this book demonstrates examples of "typical" import transactions. Usually, first orders follow the "Murphy's Law" of importing. There are often glitches, such as delivery delays (as I've mentioned before, most foreign countries do not work on "Amcrican Time"), initial prototype and production quality modifications, weather-related issues (monsoons, typhoons, etc.), all of which are normally easily remedied with advance scheduling and planning, allowing for plenty of production time, and TONS OF PATIENCE!

About the Authors

Edith G. Tolchin

Edith G. Tolchin, "*The Sourcing Lady*" (SM), "invented" ***EGT Global Trading*** in 1997, with a goal to link U.S. inventors with Asian manufacturers, to provide a "one-stop import service" for sourcing, quality control, manufacturing, international financing, air/ocean shipping, customs clearance arrangements, and dock-to-door delivery. Edie began her career in import and international trade in 1973, fresh out of NYU, with a NYC importer of frozen fish and bicycles. She has worked with both large and small importers, handling commodities from salted nuts to chemicals and waxes, to wearing apparel and toys. Ms. Tolchin holds a U.S. Customs Broker License, and has extensive experience with U.S. Customs and Customs Brokers in various products and issues, including binding rulings, duty protests and drawbacks. She is a Professional Member of the United Inventors Association.

Ms. Tolchin currently writes a twice-weekly column, "Striking a Simple Balance" on work-life issues for the Times Herald-Record in New York, and is a contributing writer for Orange Magazine, also in New York.

EGT Global Trading specializes in offshore manufacturing services for inventions of textiles and sewn-items, bags, baby and fashion accessories, unique arts & crafts items, and household inventions. Edie Tolchin regularly provides presentations for inventors' organizations and trade shows throughout the USA on topics such as "Importing Basics for Inventors™," and "Offshore Manufacturing for Inventors™."

For free brochure and lit packet, please contact: ***EGT Global Trading***, P.O. Box 231, Florida, NY 10921 USA. Fax (845) 651-3214, e-mail: EGT@warwick.net, webpage: www.egtglobaltrading.com

Don Debelak

Don Debelak has been working with new products and inventions for over 25 years and is the author of four of the best-known invention books of the last 15 years. He also was the author or Entrepreneur Magazine's Bright Idea column on inventions for over seven years. Don has spent his career

marketing products for new and small businesses, writing numerous business plans for raising money, both from investors and banks. Don has worked with all types of business, especially as a consultant for the University of St. Thomas Small Business Center, from small one man service business to high-tech ventures that are set up to raise money and launch a new product.

www.DonDebelak.com is an inventor assistance site run by Don Debelak with the help of other marketers and product engineers. The site is dedicated to help inventors who want to market their own product, find cost effective ways to make prototypes, prepare complete engineering drawings and documentation, and manufacture low volume production.

Other services include product introduction plans, marketing and business plans as well as one-on-one consulting. Don also provides market penetration assistance for international inventors by preparing action plans and sales and marketing assistance.

Eric Debelak

Eric Debelak has been working with Don Debelak and DonDebelak.com since 2004. He is the Editor of the popular DonDebelak.com Newsletter, a free bimonthly newsletter with lots of free help for inventors, and has been the driving force behind DonDebelak.com's Catalog Marketing Program that has sold over $500,000 of products in its first two years.